THE LONGEST YOU'VE LIVED ANYWHERE

Poems

New & Selected 2013

Bruce Taylor

UPRIVERPRESS

A fool on a fool's errand would be a fool to stop.

> Kurt Vonnegut, Jr.
> *Sirens of Titan*

for Patti, still
& for Charlie Bass

Acknowledgements:

Abraxus, , Gulf Coast, The Anglican Theological Review, The Chicago Review, The Chicago Tribune, The Courtland Review, The Cumberland Review, The Exquisite Corpse, The Formalist, Greensboro Review, The Hamline Journal, Hayden Ferry Review, The Journal, Light, Literary Salt, The Little Magazine, Madison Review, The Midwest Review, The Nation, The New York Quarterly, The New Orleans Review, New Works Review, NG, The Northwest Review, Passages North, Poetry Magazine, Poetry Northeast, Poetry Now, Porcupine, Rattle, RE-Verse, Slow Trains, South Florida Review, The Texas Review, Verse Wisconsin, The Wisconsin Academy Review, The *Writer's Almanac,* and *Your Daily Poem.*

"Calling it the Given," "Like," "Arabesque," and "Gray Drapes" first appeared in *Poetry* © 1994 by the Modern Poetry Association.

Poems and earlier versions of poems from this collection have also appeared in *Everywhere the Beauty Gives Itself Away*, Red Weather Press, 1976; *Idle Trade: Early Poems*, Wolfsong Press, 1979; *This Day,* Juniper Press, 1993; *Why That Man Talks That Way*, Upriver Press, 1994; *Pity the World*, Plainview Press, 2005.

Cover by Jane Cooper
Cover Photo by Patti See

Copyright © 1976, 1979, 1982, 1984, 1993, 1994, 2005, 2012, 2013 Bruce Taylor

EVERYDAY 1

    OUR BODY 2
    YESTERDAY'S POEM 3
    ANOTHER POEM YOU TRY TO READ 4
    THEME MUSIC 5
    EVERYDAY 6
    ALMOST WINTER 7
    THE LONGEST YOU LIVED ANYWHERE 8
    YOUR RETIRING MIND 9
    IN CLASS EXERCISE 10
    THOSE DRINKING DAYS 11
    ANOTHER POEM IN PROGRESS 12
    IN THE MORNING GARDEN 13
    AT MIRROR LAKE 14
    WHAT A DAY 15
    LITTLE ELEGIES: 9 PM 16
    FAST FACTS ABOUT FAMOUS PEOPLE 18
    WHAT? 19
    AS IS 20
    REALITY CHECK: AT THE WRITER'S CONFERENCE 21
    A "MUG'S GAME" 22
    TRAVEL ADVISORY 23
    MIDDLED-AGED MAN, SMOKING 24
    NEXT DOOR 26
    WHAT TO DO NEXT 27
    YEARS 28
    WHAT EVERYONE KNEW AND DIDN'T 29
    WHAT HE DOESN'T KNOW ABOUT HER 30
    YOUR BASIC FEMALE BODY 31
    FRIDAYS 32
    TOMATO 33
    ASKING SUM 34
    POETRY SEX LOVE MUSIC BOOZE & DEATH: 36
    "WHAT A STRANGER MIGHT CONSTRUE" 38
    SAINT BRUCE 40

from ***These Days*** *42*

    SUNDAY 43
    BLANKET WEATHER 44
    NEXT DOOR, SPRING 45
    OUR BACK YARDS 46
    JANUARY: SUNNY AND COLD: THE BUS 47
    MIDDLE-AGED MEN, LEANING 48
    WEDNESDAY, THE HOLE 50
    SUNDAY, THE ORDEAL 51
    HUMMING THE 'B' SIDES 52
    ANOTHER YEAR, THE BIRDS 53

from ***Living Like Thugs*** *55*

    SINGING "THE STONES" 56
    MIDDLE-AGED MAN, WALKING 57
    WHAT THEY CAN AND CANNOT FAKE 58
    WHAT THEY HAVE AND HAVE NOT 59
    ALMOST DANCING 61
    HIS UNCLE PEARL 62
    THAT KIND OF A GUY 64
    HIS FATHER BEFORE HIM 65
    HIS GOOD FELT HAT 66

from ***This Day*** *68*

    FOREIGNER 69
    THE WINDOW 70
    GRAY DRAPES 71
    CALLING IT THE GIVEN 72
    LIKE 73
    PATHETIQUE 74
    AFTER BONNEFOY 75
    THE GUEST ROOM 76
    THEN 77
    STROPHE 78
    FOR DANCING 79

EVERYDAY
>One light in a window
is enough to bring the whole shore to life.
>
>Gaston Bachelard

OUR BODY

It's too heavy
in the early morning
too easy to lay down
lightly late at night.

If this were only bigger
and this smaller,
if these were like that
and that was blond.

If this could be longer
harder, sharper,
if that weren't so soft,
so palpable and moist.

If only it didn't fill
and empty, didn't ache
so sometimes to be held
and others to be let go.

YESTERDAY'S POEM

regrets everything,
is strangled by circumstance,
mourning and wishing
and wondering why.

I used to love yesterday's
poem, all echo and hindsight
trailing the little that was
left of not that long ago,

a record of the gone beyond
all I thought said and done,
it seemed to be everything
there was to say, at the time.

For instance this cup
of half cold coffee half full
and the shadow of that birch
tossed upon another page

the waves of course
and if not that gull
another hovering
just hovering.

ANOTHER POEM YOU TRY TO READ

but wake in a surprising shade,
your glasses still on barely
and the book spread open
across your grumbling belly.

The cat in a coma across your feet
the dog dreaming in the coming chill
fridge whining, furnace complaining,
the pine outside your window still

last you knew full of morning and song,
a long shadow leading to a setting sun.
The last line you read you try in
the gathered dusk to read again.

THEME MUSIC

that song you heard one
midnight walking, the one
about dancing, that made you
wish you had been recently

or that bluesy little ditty
scatted slightly off key,
you'd whistle it if you could,
in your head all morning now.

Or a hymn our fathers hummed,
hoeing their own hard rows,
the amen when we rest
hallelujahs as we rise again,

the half-forgotten lullaby for
children missing, lost and gone,
the old moon with the new moon
nearly hushed in its arms.

EVERYDAY

The first cold morning you've
already brought in wood
for the fire you finally need.

The rainy morning when
you can't do what you have to
so you can do what you want.

The raining again morning
when you can't do what you
love so you do what you can.

The fourth morning she's gone,
the one before the one she
returns home again to you.

The morning you wait all
the long night for, your one
small light visible for miles.

ALMOST WINTER

Your windows caulked, washed,
locked and sealed in plastic,
your two sturdy new shovels
and a hundred pounds of sand.

Your lights stay on all day under
these kinds of skies, the birds
in chill good riddance, have gone
further south this year, earlier.

You blow hard on your hands,
beat your hands to your breast,
wipe your nose on your gloves,
quick step briskly in place.

You nail a blanket to the door.
It starts to begin to maybe snow.

THE LONGEST YOU LIVED ANYWHERE

The way an almost autumn morning
comes to south facing houses
on the far side of the river,
slow along a low bank sculpted
by an August afternoon,

from a window where you always sit
a view from the second story,
the slightly bigger picture
of the smallness of your life.

Time passing not so much
as staying and settling,
the dead float of an old boat
adrift in the leaves, the crawl

of the shadow of a hoe aslant
the garage wall, a guilty thing
surprised by the slowness of its shame.

YOUR RETIRING MIND

Lug cat food in the front,
kitty litter out the back.
Envy the fish's dozy float.
Turn down the thermostat,

the radio on and TV off.
Cover the bird, let in the dog.
Close all the blinds pull down
the shades. Lock the door.

Is someone standing there
this evening knocking too
softly to get in? Was anybody
coming, or even expected to?

Pour one more last drink.
Stare into the fridge again.
Leave the dishes in the sink.
Wonder if it's going to rain.

IN CLASS EXERCISE
My Hand Is Sad When ...

it is not with your hand,
tapping at a polished table top
tuning out and away from
any happy song on the radio.

It thinks *why try*
and sulks in its pocket
drinks too much coffee,
stirs, trembles

at the shapes it makes
longing to reach for you,
at the way it is always
waving to you goodbye

cradling my saddest face,
smoking my breath away,
idling lightly across some
white unbothered page.

THOSE DRINKING DAYS

To those lovers
who people impossibly
the possible world
in whose arms all
ideal passions rise

to whose fierce kiss
the sensible world
throws back its head
and bares its neck
and cries

to whose slow touching
under stars whose
nowhere walking
arms around waists
whose starry eyes

whose whiskey lips
and staggering embrace
the sleeping world
stirs in its dreaming
and sighs.

ANOTHER POEM IN PROGRESS

reminds us that life is short
and the world is filling up
with time. True, you may not

step in the same stream twice
but every day I watch from my same
place this street at this same

time. True yesterday's Chevy
with a broken taillight's today's
Ford with a headlight missing,

and maybe the barkeep sweeps or
is sweeping or has already swept
his sidewalk and then scattered

the seed for the sparrows in
the initials of someone he knows
who needs this simple prayer.

Of course, yesterday's girl isn't
getting any younger, but do we old men
sigh less when she crosses our minds?

IN THE MORNING GARDEN

I wish you could have been with me
this morning in my garden or what
I call a garden or what I call mine

when the garden called me this morning
down the 11 stairs to the quiet kitchen,
last night's coffee gone cold in the pot,

where I sat and scribbled nothing
with the radio on scattering my ashes,
smoking what's left of my breath away,

out the ragged, rusty hinged screen door
I let go slat and bang behind me, down
into what I call a garden, the icy dew ankle

deep in the grass, and with it the ache
for you I wake with, all the light early
and slant, all the birds about to sing.

AT MIRROR LAKE

The sun rises from its depth
to set the world on fire,
water overflows with clouds
thirsting for rain.

Tops of trees shimmer still
following the current light
rootless in the shallows
where the sky edges the shore.

Two lone boats doze and float
the morning, misty as it settles,
the same old man, the same dog,
another day the world allows.

WHAT A DAY

What a morning
rising and breaking in
that sky like that again,

clouds birds trees,
our familiar surprises,
waters still, pooling

and lunch, just what you
wanted, just how you like it
and when, exactly right.

Nothing to do the whole long
afternoon so full of
the nothing you planned.

Evening evening evening lovely
to call it that, languid,
languishing even as it passes.

LITTLE ELEGIES: 9 PM

"local tavern burns, news at eleven"

Tipsy Donna in many
and large polka dots
out of the cab home
from the 5 o' clock Club
after work every day
will come stumbling up
her walk or sometimes
ours somewhere around
seven, seven-thirty, no more.

Neither will Lightfoot,
his real name, and a burden
one would assume
for a guy with a clubfoot,
peddle shines & smutty
limericks from his usual
stool at the end of the bend
of the bar at the Elbow Room,
gone a long time now.

Nor is the guy in the sandals
and the white ten gallon
Texas Stetson who walks
the big white chow
on twelve feet of clothesline,
rain, glare-ice, or shine across
the abandoned railroad trestle
toward the old New Home
likely to be heading any longer.

Neither will Rhett, as he prefers
to be called, a tattooed ferret
of a Vietnam vet
and his most beautiful wife
in her customized wheelchair
—chopped it himself—
towards or away from
Big June's Treadmill be
coming and going anytime soon.

FAST FACTS ABOUT FAMOUS PEOPLE

Pol Pot liked a good laugh.
Mussolini got the trains to run on time.
Hitler wept at the opera.

Miro hated green beans
Picasso beets.
Chagall both beets and beans.

Dickens slept facing north.
Longfellow was the first
American to have indoor plumbing.

Abraham Lincoln had no middle name.
Caesar was a pretty good swimmer.
Mao was an assistant librarian.

Churchill washed his own socks.
Bell never phoned his mother.
Edison was afraid of the dark.

WHAT?

it is is what it boils down
to, what's up & what's going
down. It's where it is and
when. The matter and the deal,
the angle, the game the score
the price, the scoop the skinny,
the number trouble problem.
What women want or what man
hath wrought, the difference
a day makes, what the doctor
ordered, your poison, wish and
pleasure, the odds, the word.
It's next, it's new, what you
know or don't or think you do
that may or may not hurt you.
What you feel, mean, make, think
have, have not or gave it up for,
happened, lost and still remains.
A waste, a way to go, a relief.

AS IS

The whine when you start up.
The leak in the bottom.
The grunt when you stop.
That stain you'd forgotten.

The scratch in the back.
The flaw design foretold.
The mend, the fix, the patch
that might or might not hold.

The repairs you live with
beyond any warranty.
The human error intrinsic
your only guarantee.

The clutch in the gut or the chest.
The lump in the throat or the breast.

REALITY CHECK: AT THE WRITER'S CONFERENCE
for the Sisters Karamazov

A Porsche in the parking lot
with a vanity plate, "IAMB,"
a Bentley by the conference center
which used to be the barn.

There's a slim, bikini'd
prose-poet Tai Chi-ing while
the tractor circles around him
cutting lawn for volleyball.

They're grazing salad bars
while discussing Amy Lowell.
They're jogging up and down
the Robert Frost Trail.

Conversations and choices
croak with irony and wit
to write some poetry or attend
yet another lecture about it.

Outside, stars each to each
inspire and are inspired by.
Inside, the registration fee
is nonrefundable by July.

A "MUG'S GAME"

The faster you want it, the slower it comes,
so says the Bard and the Bard ought to know,
the smaller the insect, the larger the crumb.

What you hold is what you must let go.
The less you keep the more you need.
So says the Bard and the Bard ought to know.

The harder you struggle to succeed
the likelier you are to stumble and fall.
The less you keep, the more you need

to want to not let go and keep it all,
a staggering weight under which
the likelier you are to stumble and fall.

The starry nights no longer astonish,
the empty days fill slowly up with woe,
a staggering weight under which

the empty days fill slowly up with woe.
The faster you want it, the slower it comes
so says the Bard and the Bard ought to know,
the smaller the insect the larger the crumb.

TRAVEL ADVISORY

Don't go, don't leave where
you are for where you're not,
this here for that there,
what you know for what you don't.

You won't eat the food,
you can't drink the water.
Do you even know the word
for *bathroom* or *beer*?

Don't get on that plane.
Let the ship sail without you.
You won't ever miss the train,
if you never leave the station.

You'd always be lost there.
No one knows what you like
and how and when and how
often with what else.

How will you pack what
you forgot you'll need?
In what do you carry what
you can't ever do without?

MIDDLED-AGED MAN, SMOKING

It's way too late for a guy your age to be out
and the only store for miles about
has closed and you had your last cigarette
an hour ago hanging around the ashtrays at
the bus station with nowhere to go in your life

and your girlfriend resents you and your wife
remembers what you used to be and your children
are cruising planet Reebok and your foreman
is a prick and they raised Black Jack a dime
a shot and you got warts and a bunion
and two golf ball sized cysts on your ass

and somewhere you heard since the last
you knew they've found six or eight planets
a couple of whole solar systems, a secret
previously unknown life form that lives on
methane, good intentions and nicotine.

"This friggin country," you find yourself saying
lately, or "When I was your age," betraying
more than you want or used to, and too much
whiskey makes you want to talk too much
which is one good reason you drink it,
you got no time anymore for lawn care or irony

or auto repair or power walking or even dignity
but there's a poofy haired blond at the curb
parked in a rusty Celebrity playing Herb
Alpert on her 8 track and a half a pack of Old Golds
shimmering on the dashboard and you know

an afterhours place about a mile or two away
out by the airport down on County Highway
Q where you might get a little credit
and the bouncer, the big one, is a real sweetheart
you think his name's Ray, or maybe Raoul,
works every weekend, smokes Luckies too.

NEXT DOOR

A guy on his own roof looking down
who you can barely stand to watch
as he teeters closer to the edge
and peels some rotting shingles off
crooked as he is, all askew
at many angles irreversibly
sloping towards disaster,
not that high really, maybe,
but high enough.

"Guy about your age," your nurse
of an ex-wife always began a story
and you know you're in for it then,
"fell two feet off a stepstool
while changing a bulb and will
never walk, or anything, again."

Typical, you think, supper time
talk, until the overhead light
in the kitchen sputtered and blew,
and you knew she knew you'd sit
in the dark the rest of the night
and smoke and drink and think.

WHAT TO DO NEXT

What you meant to but forgot
what you tried but couldn't
what you really wanted to a lot
what you thought you shouldn't.

All the good things you planned
every right thing you know
this thing here close at hand
that old thing from long ago.

What you never bothered to
get around to so goes undone
what it's almost too late to
or what you've just begun.

What you were thinking yesterday
whatever you remembered then
you put somewhere intentionally
so you'd never misplace it again.

Whatever the season might ask
whatever the day will bring
what's next to last or last
a walk, maybe a nap, or nothing.

YEARS

had passed without a visit or a call
but the short, chatty scrawl
of a note, twice a year, or a card
that was particularly hard
to choose, and the small
but thoughtful gifts, late, as usual,
but always there and no one
could ever wait to open them.
You brought your sons to your father
to learn to love each other
as you had learned to love them,
son by father, father by son.
First they were shy the way men
have learned to be shy when
they begin to love one another,
faced the best worst face the other
could make, told stories, laughed
and took way too many photographs
wanting each moment flashing past
to stay, at least a while, to last
beyond a family's fond remembrance
they had, as it turned out, only once.

WHAT EVERYONE KNEW AND DIDN'T

In every bar on the street
everyone knew what they drank,
exactly which day of the week
it is by where it was they sat,

in which dark booth indiscrete
laughing loud, heads thrown back
under the emollient neon halos'
strobed and stridulated afterglow.

They went everywhere together
they could get away with going,
didn't quite burn but did smolder,
didn't dance but did tiptoe

side by side, shoulder to shoulder.
It wasn't easy but was easy going
as love is impeded but requited,
forlorn perhaps, but not forfeited.

Everyone knew or thought as well
so no one asked and they didn't tell.

WHAT HE DOESN'T KNOW ABOUT HER

What songs does she hum in the garden?
What does she wear when she's sick
or when she washes the floor?
How does she sound complaining?
What does she do when she's bored?

Where does she go to be alone?
What song does she sing to her children?
What does she say to her husband
when he asks how was her day?
What does she look like walking away?

YOUR BASIC FEMALE BODY

– accessorized –

garter belt, crinoline, camisole,
bustier, bustle and brassiere,
chemise and spike heel, nose ring,
veil, kid glove, fishnet stockings,
fichu bangled, bandeau beaded,
diamond choker, boa of endangered fur
or one sloppy sock and tattered scanty,
milky gloss of jeans or slip of a wrist
beneath a worn work shirt or a pulse
of jugular beneath a family cameo,
or acne and cyst and dangerous mole
her flawless back adorn, small
unexplainable scars, bruise you dare
not speak of, a mark of a hand,
trace of time's line around
the girl of her eyes.

FRIDAYS

Afterwards, they're too used to it all
to weep anymore in a parking lot
at such a normal thing as parting,
birds coming or going, all the trees
putting off or on their leaves.
There's the usual weekend errands,
he gets kitty litter and light bulbs,
she salmon and trash-bags. What they are
expected to bring home and what they do.
Then there's the left turn and the right,
the predictable nature of the antipodal,
while the lights in every direction,
at every intersection blink their easy advice—
to stop or go or to proceed with caution.

TOMATO

He had spotted it earlier that afternoon
and when she went to the garage
to get another bottle of wine
he went to the garden and picked it.
The first of the season, the earliest
they'd ever had one, the size of his fist
and so ready-ripe they had to eat it
in a bowl. "Food of the Gods," she said
as she sliced the tomato like a side of beef
and devoured each slice in two salacious bites.
It was the first thing they had said for an hour
that wasn't racked with regret and pain.
The daughter interrupted the most
that long August afternoon, dowsing
towards twilight, sensing something, whiny
and clinging to her mother or trying to get
the mother to come with her anywhere to do
anything that wasn't this, whatever this was,
in the dim kitchen speaking in hushed tones.
She came in once with her hairbrush
and barrettes and placed them on the table,
and then with some cards, Old Maid maybe or
Go Fish, which she called Go to the Dump
because that's what her mother called it.
She came in and out many other times,
straight-arming the swinging door,
the worried dog ever vigilant at her heels.

ASKING SUM

So what does that say?
I ask, pointing far beyond
the waves of palm and mango

and other trees I cannot name,
towards a stream of rainbow neon
washing across the South China skies.

It says singing here, he says,
*it says music and dancing
and friends you will find there.*

And what about that, even a little
further away, even more blurry
in the heat and distance?

A bank. Sum says. *It says your money here.*
And that, further still almost just a flicker
of blue green, almost too far too see?

I don't know, Sum says,
*I think it is selling something
but I don't know what.*

And how many people live
here in Zhuhai? I ask.
Nobody knows, he says

and he's right of course.
Nobody ever does. And what is
making that noise there

in the woods, we would say
it sounds like moose or platypus
if platypus made a sound,

or any moose lived here,
but he doesn't get the joke.
And I never see anybody

mow a lawn but the grass
is always perfect
and why does no one jog

and why in so large a city
do I never hear any sirens?
Sum doesn't know.

And why does every bridge
announce how long it is
before you cross it,

and what does the button,
marked "Fuzzy," on the washing
machine really do?

Sum says he knows but cannot say.

POETRY SEX LOVE MUSIC BOOZE & DEATH

A "Lite" Sestina

He liked his poetry
like he liked his sex
done for love
to soft music
with a little good booze
and rarely a thought of death.

She was dying
to show him her poem
called "Kisses Like Wine"
about that rainy night together
with Sinatra on the stereo
when she first fell in love.

He didn't know about love
it seemed like the end
of some half-forgotten song,
like some over spoken couplet
recited without passion,
so he had another bourbon.

Sometimes when he was drunk
he thought he was in love,
especially when they both came
and she had fallen asleep.
He'd read a little early Yeats,
try to find some R&B on the radio.

She preferred sonatas to Sam Cooke
and didn't really like to drink.
She had always thought poetry
ought to be all about love
that went on long after death
but never as far as "doing it."

What else is there except fucking?
he said and put on Marvin Gaye.
We're born and then we die.
Now tip your glasses high,
and love whoever is around to love
that's the way to make your life a poem.

So they balled until they ran out of booze
and all the tunes were love songs.
What then was left? Just poetry and death.

"WHAT A STRANGER MIGHT CONSTRUE"

Time was a son would pay a father's debts,
keep close to ease a father's dying,
have sons himself to teach and understand
how to let go without regret
of everyone we love, one at a time
or all at once, that mystery.

This is another time, so little mystery
I am a son who hasn't honored my debt
to your sacrifice, all your lost time.
I lived so you could start your dying
and here's the usual regret,
a lack of touch or talk enough to understand.

Your rage and absences I tried to understand,
your weakness seemed a mystery,
the early marriage and the late regret.
The job you hated but it paid the debts
paid weekly for your daily dying.
You spent yourself in time.

Early to an empty bed to rise on time
you woke to sunless rooms. I understand
the crush of sequence now, how months go dying
into years, the lack of mystery.
How the future's looming unengendered debts
infect the past with a cancerous regret.

The past is over. We go beyond regret
to put each other at ease. It's time
to honor you though honor pays no debts
as doesn't praise you wouldn't understand.
Why we did what we did remains a mystery
unsolved by either of our dyings.

I wasn't there to ease you in your dying.
We die alone and that we all regret,
pass from mystery unto mystery,
our clockwork hearts on borrowed time
live just long enough to understand
to whom we owe and why the heavy debt.

Debts we dread to owe the most, in time
get paid without regret. Sons grow to understand
the living in the dying, the father's mystery.

SAINT BRUCE

> *As Stephen who looked to heaven and prayed*
> *into thy mercy all innocents accept,*
> *and as James, the Reconciler,*

of all who are at variance and enmity,
live and reign forever in heaven with thee,
Oh Lord of the vagrant, out of luck and time,
accept into thy glorious host
the victim of victims, the latest divine—

patron of the middle-aged, mediocre
and common, eventual protector
of procrastinators and the just obtuse—
Lord, we offer for your consecration
the sometimes, somewhat holy, St. Bruce

who went almost daily his daily rounds
doing little good he knew but less harm
or at least he often wanted to believe
as much as one does and can amidst
your basically unverifiable verities.

Suffering? I'll tell you he suffered,
the usual debts, second-guesses, rebuffs,
doubts and regrets, your ordinary
and customary slings and arrows,
the regularly scheduled irregularities.

He survived though, and that any of us do,
to struggle love and try—or bother to—
seems enough for a saint or a sinner,
your obvious everyday miracle,
your usual loser as daily bread winner.

So cut him some slack, Lord, give him a break,
it's the right thing to do for Jesus' sake
who lived not "long" as the old curse goes
but lived, you ask us to believe, at all
a life like this, then died, and still arose.

from *These Days*

> We lived for days on only food and water.
> W.C. Fields.

SUNDAY

Nobody goes to church much anymore,
though no one does much of anything else
so it's quiet, or as quiet as it gets;

usually there's a saw or somebody's mower,
a drill or a hammer hating another
repair we will have to live with

and the rare home run from the ballpark
and the pulse and trailing whisper
of the sprinklers when it's dry

and old deaf Winslow's blind
old cocker spaniel winds itself up
short around the clothes pole again

and the soft—almost apologetic—
screen door's screech and slam,
the trash can's guilty clatter after dark.

BLANKET WEATHER

Burrowing deeper into bed
beneath quilts and comforters,
blankets, flannel sheets and spreads,
we breathe and dream

enduring the level stare
of the red fox frozen in its den,
tracks that follow you everywhere
through an immaculate silence

days too blue to breathe
that sometimes go so clear
you begin to believe
you can skate them,

nights, 30 below and falling,
if you move they ring like bells,
out there other lives are calling
we know are worse than ours.

NEXT DOOR, SPRING

The kid's two this year
and in a neon-pink snow parka
for although it is April
it's April in Wisconsin.

Her snow pants are maroon
and large enough for three
so she squats when she sits,
it would be too easy to say,
like some surprising flower
amongst the drying piles
of last November's leaves.

But her grandmother does
plant her in the saffroned lawn,
and go inside a moment.
Someone is always watching here
from a stoop next door or through
a window from across the alley.

And when she comes back,
pointing at a robin shivering
on a frozen clothesline,
and when she says "Spring,"
to the child blooming before her,
she's right of course.

Even in here, behind the grimy
storm-windows, even the inside plants
hunched in corners and clinging to
their few handfuls of dirt,
stir as if remembering.

OUR BACK YARDS

all face each other here so
whatever we have to hide we fail to.
She appears in a clean apron
among her chrysanthemums
and stands, hands on her hips,
while he reads the *Trib*
in the shade, everyone who knows
him says you'd never know
the Doctors say the cancer's worse.

Soon she is out running a wet rag
along her clothesline under a vaguely
threatening sky. Sanka in one hand,
a Lucky Strike tight in her mouth.
WAYY's on her kitchen radio
and her kitchen window's open.
September is "Nostalgia Month"
and sometimes we're almost ashamed
at how little it takes to make us happy.

JANUARY: SUNNY AND COLD: THE BUS

It's not a long walk except it's cold
but sunny, so some try it and we pass them,
huffing their shadows, hands over their ears.
No news is good news and there's no news here.

She's quite a talker, we say after she's left,
busy about a Tuesday's bills and errands
getting off where she always does
at an alley where an oil truck is usually idling.

So we talk about that all the way downtown,
a son on each coast who take turns calling
every other Sunday and her daughter married
and divorced two or three times by now.

Our stout soprano driver sings "I'm in the Mood
for Love" over cobblestone and railroad track,
her raucous vibrato across pot-hole and frost-heave
takes us where she's going, and will bring us back.

MIDDLE-AGED MEN, LEANING

four movements

They lean on rakes.
It's late, it is evening
already inside their houses.

The children are gone.
Their wives are on the phone
talking softly to someone else.

This frost, this early Fall
upon their minds, a small
measure of patience and regard

as if the twilight world
in bright papery pieces
diminished so and thus.

~

They lean on hoes
in Spring the green earth
turned once more beneath them

their eyes full of flowers
their hands full too
of the planting still to do

the weeds and drought awaiting
their pocketful of seed
the water they must carry.

~

In an early winter dark they lean
on shovels, a graying heart
a last bad rap inside them,

looking upward toward the sky
the yard, the driveway, the car
the street, the world

itself for all they know
buried by the falling snow
even as they gasp to breathe

and re-breathe the visible breath,
like a burst cartoon balloon
of an old imperfect prayer.

~

In summer, after long mowing,
they lean toward a growing
silence in the plush grasses

in leaves of many greens
in trees of their own colors
where grackle and crow

each to its own shadow
in the dusky reach of branches
gather quietly to stay.

WEDNESDAY, THE HOLE

Isn't often you see a hole dug
as deep as this one up here so
when the county came to dig it
most of the old men came around
sometime during the day to watch.

So there were usually four
or five guys standing around
watching three guys standing around
watching one guy dig, and the boss
came by twice to check, and the Power
& Light guys stopped by too.

And the kids on their trikes,
painted red white & blue,
were warned "don't get too close"
but did and it was all too much
for Happy, Ray's penned-up
husky pup, who's learned to ignore
the tomcat's strut or another
fat rabbit fattening upon
clover in the patchy lawn.

Lunchtime, the crew took their pails
to the shady side of the truck
and someone brought ice-tea
and Ray smuggled them a beer each.
Then it was back to work so
a different guy dug and Ray took
the Buick to the Super-A
for popsicles and more beer.

SUNDAY, THE ORDEAL

You forget how it can get here
but then it is August
and the pipes begin to sweat.
A fat kid tailed by his pimply sister
kicks a useless kite all up and down
another treeless street named Elm.

Or the catbird, low in the honeysuckle,
and the cat itself only half-dozing
on the garden wall by the newlyweds
next door who are no longer young,
but are close enough for this town.

Two alleys over there used to be
a mom and pop place until Pop died
and Mom boarded up the big windows,
took down the sign and went inside,
got sick and hasn't come out since.

Everything's sent in or taken out.
A hired guy from Social Welfare
does the lawn and shovels when
it snows but doesn't do the drive
and someone, maybe a son, stops by
Sundays in a cab but never stays long.

HUMMING THE 'B' SIDES

It's *Autumn in New York*
as he vacuums, since his wife's got
the day job it's the least he can do,

or *What Is This Thing Called Love*
while he waits in the mini-van
for the kids after swimming or piano.

It's *Ebb Tide* when the cat, the baby,
the fat goldfish in the algaed pond
doze and float in a lazy eddy

of a August late afternoon nap,
and *They Can't Take That Away from Me*
later still when the tin little A.M. grins

dimly in the dusk tuned faintly to
WAYY, "where every tune's a memory,
 where all the great old songs have gone."

ANOTHER YEAR, THE BIRDS

All summer long there was always
a caw, a complaint or call.
And later in the fall,
as the breathy clouds
when the wind's westerly move
endlessly away from you,
whole flocks of finch appeared
to forage in the weeds
that struggle and go to seed where
the driveway fractures and drifts,
as the continents themselves,
we are told, fracture and drift.

And in winter at 30 below,
your breath escaped you,
a white cloud across
that big morning star
like one singular and rare
chrome wind chime's note,
then a door far off slams so
another does then a dog barks
then another then the pickups,
cars and vans in sequence startle
the heavily feathered sparrows
flocking bare lilacs along
four geometric blocks
of perfectly shoveled snow.

And then the same swallows come
back to nest in the same
inverted flower-pot painted
whatever color's handy
and nailed to a shingle
blown off the roof,
and then the trees take on
their burden again and again
we are left with almost nothing
but Spring and happiness,
the conditional joys.

from *Living Like Thugs*

> Is it hot in here or am I crazy?
> Charlie Manson

SINGING "THE STONES"

"imagining the world that I got"

A Salesman on a lucky roll
his profit is your loss.
The Dentist on a weekend prowl
his pockets full of floss.

The Grave digger out for a laugh.
The Shrink for a shoulder to cry on.
The Plumbers on time and a half.
The Bankers who never will buy one.

The Painter who knocked off early
today and may tomorrow too.
The Guys who had it made, nearly,
and Guys that don't know it but do.

The Little Guys on the tall stools.
The Fat Guys bellied up to the bar.
The Young Guys trying to be so cool
and the Old Guys so sure that they are.

MIDDLE-AGED MAN, WALKING

He knows the world is round
they said so in school
but he walks it flatly still,
an edge more than horizon.

Not as you might walk a planet
rolling around a Universe
you fear to suppose or even infer
but as you plot and replot

a trip on a map so creased
and wrinkled each section
threatens if you check it again
to fracture off into pieces.

A languid idle by the river
Summer Spring and Fall
or the Winters' trackless stroll
over one bridge and back another.

Streets that rush off to work
and come straight home
that amble to the tavern
and tangle eventually back.

The burn in the calf or the shin,
the stab in the back or the chest,
the lack of the little breath left,
the journey uphill or down.

WHAT THEY CAN AND CANNOT FAKE

Any orgasm except a real one.
True love but not a sneeze
Not at least convincingly so.
Death, as children make believe

Though never nearly long enough.
And the shape of a kiss on the lips
But not the reach nor rest of touch
That lingers just below the finger tips.

Any present fashion of desire
Lust's vogue and classic craze
But not the first loss loss requires,
Nor compassion's passion ablaze.

Not luck or the Blues, a fugue, cold sweat,
Foul fate, true tragedy or real regret.

WHAT THEY HAVE AND HAVE NOT

They have no snapshots
they might ever keep
together except the secret
fleeing ones they take

in passing neon barroom
windows or lingering
in steamy motel mirrors
on which he paints for her

in operatic opiates awash
in letters clearly enduring
the traditionally initialed heart
the tragic arrow recondite.

They are not often Saturday
mornings in the park nor on
a sinless Sunday afternoon
stroll a civil boulevard to talk.

They rarely get to shop much,
argue or nap, time's too
short to waste on anything but
how happy they can be together.

The room they move in is
just large enough for two
small windows painted shut
ugly drapes coarsely cut

somehow they make do,
her skirt a lovely puddle
on the floor by the door
where she skinned out of it

his pants dancing off the chair
"You have to stop biting me,"
she reminds him, "where it shows."
And he agrees.

ALMOST DANCING

Drunk on fine wine and the freedom to be
obvious over foreign coffees, cognac
and the just desserts of sin, it seemed in
this distant city among strangers with

all she was or was not wearing beneath
her new dress only he knowing though
anyone who watched even a giddy while
might have naughtily guessed or known by

furtive heart or remembered once the earthly
scent of motel soap and mortal pretense,
they could dance, they thought, in this place,
could nap or dine *al fresco* – do anything together

the word they've lately learned to use
for any place or time that makes them happy.
This far from home anything could happen
which is why they have to go this far

shrugging off some other life's gray array
too cheerless and heavy for a latitude
as wide and warm as this exotic parallel,
traveling on credit someone else will pay.

HIS UNCLE PEARL

was a fat man with a thin mustache,
bad teeth and a funny hat,
who read three newspapers a day
and fell asleep on the couch,

a brute with a belt
and a hell of a backhand
a big pile of shit
or a shower of gold

a skinny chicken-legged
badly balding guy with
hardly any ass at all
jogging towards the 7-11
at 10:57 for Schlitz.

The guy at the bend
of a horse-shoe bar
peeling big bills off
a wad from his pocket,
lots louder than the rest.

The gut-gone loose shooter
eight-balling for beer,
one sly eye in the pocket
of every move the barmaid makes,
he'll snag her yet upon

his hooky smile, he thinks,
"That'll Be the Day," she plays
back on the jukebox
"You Can't Always Get What You Want."
The bleary old rummy, teary

eyed in the mirror with
a couple of dollars left,
a sucker for the 'B' sides
maybe he'll play "It Happened
in Monterey," maybe "Angel Eyes,"
one more time and leave.

THAT KIND OF A GUY

that cool silver-haired old dude
in the sharp black jacket
    and a spiffy pair of shoes
in a tiny, gray and white, button-flap
    checkered cap and a pin in his lapel
who is always going somewhere
    running his errands, making the rounds

the kind of a guy has to
    draw pictures when he talks
on the back of napkin or
    scrawl something approximate
across a scrap of an envelope
    there's this letter to mail
and the Light Bill to pay

and the Buick to get gassed and washed,
    and the list his wife leaves
him every day, and he's been looking
everywhere, he says, for a little
copper washer, 'about this big,'
"OK," he's always saying, "I got
to run, I got to go." The Optimist,

the Moose or Shriner, the Foreign
Legionnaire, the Knight of Columbus,
    who's always raffling off something
collecting something for
some worthy cause or another
    selling light bulbs for the blind
or paper flowers for the sleeping dead.

HIS FATHER BEFORE HIM

was one of the quiet ones,
who spent most of his time
in the cellar or garage
from right after supper
until everyone else was asleep,
puttering around with something,
fixing this or that, fixing it again

who sat in the dark in the kitchen
with the last cold cup of coffee
and smoked and hummed and thought
with the radio on low and tuned
to somewhere far off, fading
in and out, scratchy, oddly
operatic static ridden and remote

a man who may have loved you
but never said it, a guy who meant well
but moody, bored, angry, tired, mute
in his male terror, huge,
hairlessly marbled, frontally nude,
smelling of whiskey and gasoline,
working too hard, dying too soon.

HIS GOOD FELT HAT

All dogs and children awaiting
his flat ascending steps
up the steepest hill
for miles around,
hunched over, hands deep
into the jingle of his pockets
full of keys and key chain,
change purse, small change,
hanky, subway tokens, Tums
and Lifesavers or better yet,

Chiclets, or cough-drops, or gum
he'd give some to any grandchild
who could spell his word for the day
or who had learned another verse
from Proverbs or the Psalms ,

with his good felt hat in his hand
and his jacket folded neatly
over the other shoulder,
and his always white shirt
and his pin for perfect attendance
in the too wide lapel
of his second best suit

and his braces, belt
with initialed buckle,
vest, vest-chain, fob,
collar-stays, tie-pin,
cuff-links, Parker Pen
and Pencil set, glasses case,
address book and billfold
and if it was a Sunday
his best blue suit
and his bible, the small one,
and a white boutonniere
for his mother who was dead
and the envelopes for the offering.

from *This Day*

> You are afraid whether you will rise from the dead or not, but you rose from the dead when you were born and didn't notice it.
> Boris Pasternak

FOREIGNER

See him grunt and point.
See him with his big cold
body grunt and point.

Listen to him try
to talk like a person,
the way our words turn
to rubbish in his mouth.

Who could love him,
his face, a moon, his skin
the belly of the carp.

He walks like an ox.
He looks at the smallest thing
as if it were a miracle.

What a world that must be
the world that is his
where you can't ask for food
or tell a woman she's beautiful

where you can't pray or sing
or speak drunk to the dead
or cry out in the night for help.

THE WINDOW

He chips at the salt on the sill
with a bloody nail, calls out
to passers-by who squint, look up,
agree abstractly and pass on.

Sometimes at night something weeps
inside him, something sits down
with its head in its hands
and smokes and stares.

A craving the color of morning
spirals within him,
its terraces are of conch and whelk,
its palms are open to the sun.

Who has unfolded this linen of dream
age and patience, this bay
open to the night?

GRAY DRAPES

Gray drapes the shutterless room
when the sun goes beveling
the day we'd try to understand
even if we lived forever,
the moment we cling to
because it is our own.

The hand drawn more absently
towards pain, a flawless gesture,
floats or seems of itself no token.
Something goes on beyond the body,
that the body can believe,
the body knows itself, it fails.

Fear is the body's, fool,
the mind alone would go
anywhere, do anything.

Longing too is of the body,
the shape a hand makes, letting go,
the mouth slack, lips parted slightly.

CALLING IT THE GIVEN

full of quiet and regard

The past you thought
would be over by now

a clamor in the heart
a paradise of ruins

its only regret is
it made you what you are

what used to be called
the future of the past

where the edges of the day
wear the day away to

the many worlds you
wake through towards

the world you'll wake in
in a moment.

LIKE

a grief that one can cherish
or the dream aroused
the terrestrial version

the meaning and insinuation
of the signs of morning in
an eastern sky

a negative of the beautiful
or a movie of the future
running in reverse

of the shadow of the supple
apple saplings thrown
across the chop of shallow water

a leaf or a mountain
or the predictable horizon rising
to the repeatable moon.

PATHETIQUE

There is the sigh
that is too much
to do at work
he brings it home

it eats from the pan
with the only
clean spoon
more than its share,

the sigh of the stew
of the onion
in its many skins

the sigh of bone
as it simmers
the many blind
and buried
sighs of potatoes.

AFTER BONNEFOY

I am surprised it took this long
for the fruit was in the tree
and the flat, nomadic light was
already leaning towards leaving.

Already the evening was easing
out of its shell - its eyes amber,
its chambered and fossorial heart.

Let painters have their first light,
a light like this unhinges us.
Prey to fever and incense ascending,
white bird off in high suspense
—light of evident things.

What's the soul without its flaws?
A moment without its
knowledge of death, unthinkable.

Sometimes it goes so clear in you
you can picture it
the slow nocturnal trellis' crawl,
a tractable past
which soothes you or does not

the day and the body that
the dead, if they awaken,
awaken singing.

THE GUEST ROOM

Even without their story told,
more than a knickknack
here and there, a spoiled antimacassar,
some dried milkweed and dusty cattail
steeping for how long in a lidless teapot
a mysterious brew of nostalgia or regret,
or driftwood cast up on what huge tides
to settle here in winter on a prairie farm,
or grandfather's watch, stopped
ten minutes from now, how many untold
years ago?   A damp cloth across a dusty
aspidistra, a half-finished sampler,
"Oh Bear Me Away on Your Snowy Wings."

THEN

A vestigial
sadness astonishes
the fordable evening

someone taps
abstractly at the dial
of a luminous watch

the river falls
to other pools
other afternoons

what accident
a double cry goes out
what lunatic chore

small arms unmoored
by desire set out
upon an opposite shore.

STROPHE

By talons
it takes us
no matter where
we wander
how we wait
there is this
further blue
our longing
awakes in.

We think it quick
it is not it is
slow, a nest,
the deeper
the repose
the more emerges,
vast migrations
gather at this height.

FOR DANCING

Trembling in sympathy
unstroked by the bow
not the string played but
the string next to it

not music but what
in music makes us
wish we were dancing

in the present arms
of not forgotten lovers
whose sweep and purl
as midnight disappears

whose glide like that
lightly out of control
breathlessly unaware of
ability and will

whose reach of flesh
under fabric whose wanton
body of a beautiful youth
ever eager in our arms.

Bruce Taylor, Professor Emeritus, University of Wisconsin-Eau Claire, is the author of seven collections of poetry, and editor of eight anthologies including *Wisconsin Poetry*, and, with Patti See, *Higher Learning: Reading and Writing about College*. His poetry and translations have appeared in such places as *Able Muse, The Chicago Review, The Columbia Review, The Cortland Review, The Formalist, The Nation, The New York Quarterly, Poetry, Rattle, Rosebud* and *Writer's Almanac*.

He has won awards and fellowships from the Wisconsin Arts Board, Fulbright-Hayes, the National Endowment for the Arts, the National Endowment for the Humanities, the Council of Wisconsin Writers, and the Bush Artist Foundation.

He lives in Lake Hallie, Wisconsin with his wife, the writer Patti See.

http://www.uwec.edu/taylorb/

Printed in Great Britain
by Amazon